# Great Ice Race

Haydn Middleton

Ginn

# The Last Place on Earth

The year is 1910. Most of the Earth has been explored, but one vast continent is still a mystery: icy Antarctica, at the foot of the world. It's a cold, weird place where the temperature never gets as *high* as freezing point! For six months each year there's hardly any sun; for six months there's hardly any dark. Yet in 1910, two teams of explorers set out for the very heart of Antarctica – the South Pole. One team is British, the other is from Norway. Which team will win the race to the Pole? Will they both survive to tell the tale?

Antarctica is one and a half times as big as the USA, and the South Pole lies at its centre.

As you chase after the explorers, write down and keep your answers to each **QUIZ** question. (Remember, the answers are in the book!) And wrap up warm!

# The Race Course

## Meet the Skippers

*The all-important leaders of the British and Norwegian teams*

PAGES 6 TO 9

## On Your Marks ...

*The journey from Europe to the shores of Antarctica*

PAGES 10 TO 13

# Get Set ...

The British team's setbacks on the starting blocks

PAGES 14 TO 15

# Go!

They're off – and the race across the frozen wilderness is finally on.

PAGES 16 TO 21

# Pole Position

Who wins the great race? Find out here!

PAGES 22 TO 25

# The Final Stretch

Will both teams get home safely from the Pole?

PAGES 26 TO 31

# Meet the Skippers

Roald Amundsen comes from the cold, snowy mountain country of Norway. He always wanted to be an explorer, so he's been on many expeditions to the frozen Arctic (around the North Pole) and the Antarctic – where he once spent a whole winter! Amundsen has gobbled up any information he can find about the distant South Pole until – by 1910 – he is ready to try to lead a team all the way there.

## FiTNeSS FaCT

Amundsen has poor eyesight. That should stop him getting in the Army as a young man. But the Army doctor is so amazed at the size of his MUSCLES from working out, he forgets to give him an eye test!

Amundsen is 38 years old when he leads the Norwegian team in the Great Ice Race.

On his travels at the frozen North Pole, Amundsen has picked up useful tips from the local 'Inuit' people. They use underwear made of reindeer fur, for example. The underwear is light and warm, but lets the air circulate. Perfect pants for a trip to the South Pole!

Robert Scott is 42 years old and a captain in the British Navy. He is already famous for leading a team into unknown Antarctica, in 1900. Like Amundsen, he is tough, brave and very determined. He dreams of winning everlasting fame as the first team leader to reach the South Pole. That will mean tramping 750 miles across Antarctica, then back again. And he will have to take all his own fuel, tents, sleeping bags and cookers – along with enough food and drink for everyone. Is this man brave or **JUST PLAIN CRAZY?**

## CAPTAIN SCOTT'S LOG

*Winter 1902*

*When I was a boy, my parents were worried about the sound of my heart. The doctors found it was beating in time to two short words: 'South Pole! South Pole!' From this moment it became clear that these two words were written on my heart!* **(This is a JOKE!)**

Scott is a great author as well as an explorer. In 1905, he published a best-selling book about an earlier expedition.

# On Your Marks ...

When is a race not a race? When one of the teams doesn't know it's *in* a race! Scott's team sails from Britain in June 1910 with no idea that Amundsen's team will head south too. *They* think the Norwegian ship 'Fram' is aiming for the North Pole. So do most of Amundsen's men! Only in September does Amundsen announce to them they are racing instead to the South Pole. He sends a polite message to Scott – now in New Zealand – telling him the new plan too. By early 1911, he's *ahead* of Scott in Antarctica!

## Captain Scott's Log

*22 February 1911*

*The proper, as well as the wiser, course for us is to go on as though this is not a race. To go forward and do our best for the honour of the country without fear or panic. But there is no doubt Amundsen's plan is a very serious menace to ours. He is closer to the Pole by 60 miles.*

Scott's ship 'Terra Nova' takes 65 men to Antarctica, with 19 ponies and 33 dogs to pull sledges. A hand-picked team of just 5 men will then race over the ice towards the South Pole.

Both teams build base camps on the Antarctic coast. It is impossible to reach the Pole in the dark, bitterly cold winter, but they can build up their strength and prepare for their springtime journey.

Scott's ponies need a lot of feeding, but no grass grows in Antarctica! Amundsen brings only dogs, which are quicker on snow and easy to feed on seal meat.



**QUIZ** At the start of the race, Amundsen is in t

The teams take a lot of food and fuel closer to the Pole, then build depots where it can all be stored. They will call in and use these stores on their later journeys to and from the Pole. Meanwhile they plan hard for the race ahead. 'If we are to win,' writes Amundsen, 'not a **TROUSER BUTTON** must be missing.'

### 'FRaMHeiM' FaCT

Amundsen's base camp is something else! His expert team dig caves in the Antarctic ice to make a miniature village that they call 'Framheim'. It has kitchens, a laundry, workrooms, toilets and even a **sauna**!

# Get Set ...

*Captain Scott and his team have a few setbacks as they get ready to go!*

The British team is supposed to be learning how to ski properly, but more often they just play moonlight football! Even their Norwegian instructor joins in!
What the flippin' egg am I d-d-doing here?!
Three of the team go on a midwinter mission to find Emperor Penguin eggs. They get the eggs, but their clothes freeze and they nearly die!

# Go!

In late October 1911, both teams finally set off. They know what to expect: blizzards, snowdrifts, gale-force winds, frostbite, fog, glaciers, hunger, pain, exhaustion and – if they win the race – **GLORY!** Amundsen lets each man in his team bring 9 kilograms worth of stuff, as well as his sleeping bag. This has to include: spare underwear, mittens and socks, snow goggles, a felt hat for the bright sun and face masks for low temperatures. The Norwegians aim to travel 15 to 20 miles a day, leaving them plenty of time for rest and recuperation. Sped along by their eager dogs and skis, they simply eat up the miles.

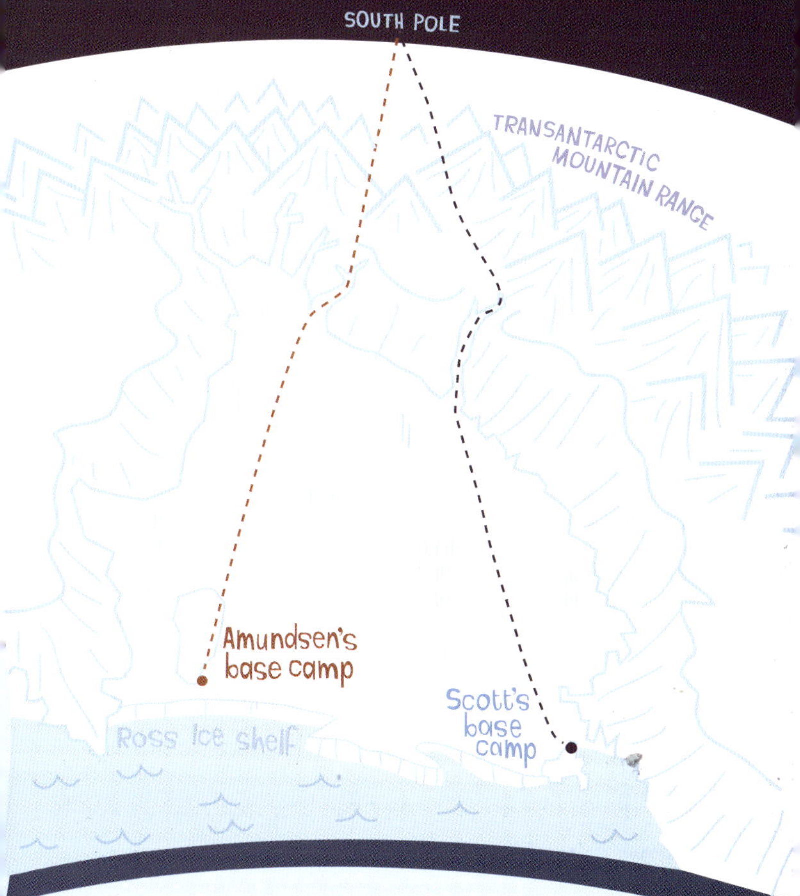


These are the routes Amundsen and Scott must take to reach the Pole. As you can see, Antarctica is not flat! Both teams will have to climb up awesome glaciers with their heavy loads. The trip there and back should take 100 days.

As the teams race on, they build more depots with supplies for their return journey. Amundsen marks his clearly with black flags, so it will be easy to pick them out amid all the snow on the way back. No man – or dog – has ever set foot – or ski – in these places before. But Amundsen has no way of knowing if Scott and the Brits are travelling faster on *their* route to the Pole.

Scott's team is finding the going pretty tough. The motor sledges soon grind to a halt, and by early December all the exhausted ponies have to be shot. Bitter storms keep the men in their tents for days on end. According to one team member, Scott has a face 'like a tired seaboot'!

**FooD FaCT**

The Norwegian team's rations aren't very tempting: biscuits, dried milk and chocolate plus 'pemmican', which is dried meat mixed with melted fat. At least there's no chance of going thirsty with all that snow to melt and drink!

On the way up a great glacier, Scott sends back his dogs. He decides that it's more reliable if the men now drag the sledges themselves. This is known as '**MANHAULING**' and it's no fun at all! Even on Christmas Day the men have to do it for 15 miserable miles!

## CAPTAIN SCOTT'S LOG

*7 January 1912*

*I found to my horror we could scarcely move the sledge on skis. The first hour was awful, owing to the wretched coating of loose sandy snow. Towards the end of our tiring march we began to make better progress, but the work is still awfully heavy.*

 Antarctica is not flat. The teams clim

The joys of manhauling. 'I have never pulled so hard,' writes one of Scott's team, 'or so nearly crushed my inside into my backbone.'

As they approach the Pole, the five Brits have no idea if the five Norwegians are ahead of them or behind. Both teams have been incredibly brave and skilful to get this far, but only one can be the first to reach the South Pole. Will it be Scott's, will it be Amundsen's – or will it be a photo finish?

# Pole Position

## Captain Scott's Log

*16 January 1912*

*The worst has happened, or nearly the worst ... This afternoon, just short of our destination, we detected a black speck ahead. Soon we knew that this could not be a natural snow feature. We marched on, found that it was a black flag tied to a sledge bearer; near by the remains of a camp; sledge tracks and ski tracks going and coming and the clear trace of dogs' paws – many dogs. This told us the whole story. The Norwegians have beaten us and are first at the Pole.*

*The moment of truth: Scott's team finds Amundsen's tent at the Pole. 'Great God!' writes Scott that night, 'This is an awful place.'*

The Brits fight their way through foul weather to the Pole – only to find the Norwegians have been and gone already! The tent they left behind proves it. Desperately disappointed, Scott's men plant a British flag too, take some scientific measurements and a few photos, then turn around and head for home. It's going to be a long hard journey back.

The Great Ice Race winner
– Roald Amundsen. It's
16,000 miles from Norway
to the South Pole, but
now – at the very bottom
of the world – the only
way is up!

## Fast Fact

When Amundsen reaches the Pole, he is a whole month and 360 miles ahead of Scott! And only nine days after Scott reaches the Pole, Amundsen is back at his own base camp!

As Scott's team returns from the Pole, Amundsen and his men, with their 39 surviving dogs, are sailing away from Antarctica. In Australia they break the news of their stunning victory. 'The whole world has now been discovered!' declares the *New York Times*. The winning Norwegians are heroes everywhere – even in Britain, where most people so badly wanted Scott to win! But where are Scott and his men? Amundsen writes that for his own team 'the whole thing went like a dream'. For Scott's team, however, everything is now turning into a **NIGHTMARE** …

# The Final Stretch

Scott's team has problems. Winter is closing in fast and the terrible weather slows them down. Without dogs to pull the sledge, they struggle to get from one supply depot to the next. Sometimes they have to go short of food and fuel and *that* makes manhauling even tougher. Tired and frostbitten, they lose their way, have accidents and get injured. One man, Edgar Evans, falls so ill that, to everyone's despair, he cannot keep going.

A photo of the Brits at the South Pole.
Back row (left to right): Oates, Scott, Evans.
Front row (left to right): Bowers, Wilson.

## Captain Scott's Log

*17 February 1912*

*We got Edgar Evans on his feet, but after two or three steps he sank down again. He showed every sign of complete collapse. Three of us went back for the sledge while Lawrence Oates remained with him. When we returned, he was practically unconscious, and when we got him into the tent, he was in a coma. He died quietly at 12.30 a.m.*

### FRoSTBiTe FaCT

When frost really gets its teeth into you, it does vile damage to your body tissues. Your nose or your feet can literally freeze up. Then nothing can be done but cut them off!

Somehow the four Brits battle on for another month – but not fast enough now. They know in their hearts they are not going to make it. Lawrence Oates is so ill, he slows the others down even more. He asks Scott to leave him outside the tent to die. Scott just urges him on. But finally Oates loses all hope.

I am just going outside and may be some time.

No one ever sees Oates again. Not long afterwards, Scott, Bowers and Wilson die in their tent. Eight months later a search party finds their bodies. It also finds Scott's log of the expedition, and a camera film that includes the photo on page 27.

A happier time for Captain Scott during the Great Ice Race. Thanks to the log he kept, we now know the story of this amazing expedition right up to its bitter end.

 **QUIZ** **Roald Amundsen from ****** was**

## Captain Scott's Log

*29 March 1912*

*Every day we have been ready to start for our depot, 11 miles away, but outside the door of the tent it remains a scene of whirling drift. I do not think we can hope for any better things now. We shall stick it out to the end, but we are getting weaker ... It seems a pity, but I do not think I can write more.*

ggle the first letters UILMGHNANA and you get MANHAULING. Arghhhhh!